D1391493

Down Your Way

Images of Hampshire's Villages

HAMPSHIRE CHRONICLE

Down Your Way

Images of Hampshire's Villages

breedon **books**
PUBLISHING

First published in Great Britain in 2005 by

The Breedon Books Publishing Company Limited

Breedon House, 3 The Parker Centre, Derby, DE21 4SZ.

A Note on the Photographs

All the photographs in the book are copyright of the Hampshire Chronicle. Copies may be ordered from the paper by calling 01962 861 860
Please quote the reference number that appears after the photograph caption.

ISBN 1 85983 498 1

Printed and bound by CPI Group, Bath Press, Avon.

Contents

Acknowledgements

Pictures by *Hampshire Chronicle* staff photographers
Terry Bond, Jon MacKintosh and Frank Riddle.

Sub-edited by Diana Hargreaves.

Foreword

LAST WINTER, just before Christmas, I drove back from a viewing, taking an alternative route down the Itchen valley through Cheriton, Tichborne, Ovington and Avington. On reaching Easton, and having driven past my childhood home, many fond memories returned. I remembered riding down to the village to watch my father play cricket, fishing in the Itchen and the village pantomime, and the idea of writing a series of articles celebrating our county's villages first came to mind.

We read on a regular basis about how sad it is to see all the village amenities disappearing – the post office that is no longer viable, the pub being converted into a house… but, as I drove through these villages, I discovered that the reality is that they are thriving and popular: Cheriton, for example, has a pub, a school, a village hall, a cricket club and a drama society, the Cheriton Players. I wondered about the feasibility of capturing the spirit of each village in a series of features for the *Hampshire Chronicle*.

'Serendipitous' was how the then *Hampshire Chronicle* publisher Paul Kinvig described our initial discussion, as he was already putting together the idea of a regular 'Down Your Way' series. The conversations that followed with ex-editor Alan Cleaver created a wonderful opportunity for Strutt & Parker and the *Hampshire Chronicle* to start working together on this interesting concept.

It was agreed that villages would be written about by both *Hampshire Chronicle* reporters and the Strutt & Parker team. For me, it was the opportunity to uproot my past: Easton was the obvious place to start, but I also recalled the NADFAS events at Stoke Charity, tennis tournaments at Preston Candover, romantic weddings at Micheldever and living at Stockbridge during my twenties. While Hampshire has been my home all my life, and I have enjoyed retracing a familiar landscape, it has also been wonderful to explore new villages.

My colleague, Emma Caulton, our publicist and an erstwhile writer and editor, whose family have lived in Hampshire for over 25 years, delighted in the chance to explore country ways and interview villagers. She visited the local inns, contemplated the past while sitting in the pretty churches and wandered down footpaths, which yielded stunning views. Together we discovered what constitutes village life today and why it continues to capture our imaginations.

We unearthed busy communities such as Droxford with its weekly produce market, established and run by locals, and Broughton with its community-run bus service and extraordinarily lengthy list of activities and societies. It has informed our working lives, too, as we now feel even better acquainted with this lovely county. Both Emma and I have thoroughly enjoyed working with the *Hampshire Chronicle* to produce both the articles in the paper and now a very exciting book, a record in pictures and words, of village life at the beginning of the 21st century. I hope you will enjoy your trip around Hampshire as much as we have enjoyed creating it.

George Burnand
Partner with Strutt & Parker's
Winchester office

Winning Waltham

LOCATED at a source of the River Hamble, this once peaceful Saxon settlement was the target of Danish raiders, a stopping-off point for the Crusades, host to innumerable royal guests at the Bishop's Palace and home town for 80 years to the Society of Missionaries of Africa.

Bishop's Waltham Palace was built by the grandson of William the Conqueror, Henri de Blois, and, although it was reduced to ruins

Bishop's Waltham has all the hallmarks of the phoenix. Whatever hand fate has dealt it in the past, it has risen from the ashes and is, today, a fascinating mix of natural features, history and specialist contemporary outlets.

under bombardment by Parliamentarian forces during the Civil War in 1644, extensive parts managed by English Heritage still offer a taste of mediaeval life. The ruins also host

The remains of the palace of the Bishop of Winchester. (T3664Q)

This attractive doorway is in Basingwell Street. (T3664L)

Householders put their best floral foot forward in Basingwell Street. (T3664K)

many community events throughout the year, including the Rotary Club Carnival and Fête. The annual Arts and Music Festival also takes full advantage of the splendid palace setting for events such as open-air Shakespeare productions and a wide range of musical events with a multi-generational appeal.

Although little trace remains today, the Houchin Street area of the town was once home to ropemakers supplying the Royal Navy. Essential to this craft was a yew post and, to commemorate the Millennium, a

St Peter's Church.
(T3664)

replica was erected by the Bishop's Waltham Society.

Admiral Villeneuve, commander of the combined Spanish and French fleets at Trafalgar, was paroled in Bishop's Waltham and stayed at the Crown in St George's Square, from where he was allowed to travel to Lord Nelson's funeral. The Admiral's lodgings were much grander than those of other French prisoners, who were kept in cages under the Market House, demolished in 1841.

The Jubilee Clock, on the site of the old Market House, was funded by public subscription to mark the Golden Jubilee of the Queen and, in summer months, is surrounded by a magnificent floral display.

The town has enjoyed a thriving commercial centre since mediaeval times and many of the buildings date from the 17th century. Some are built from oak timbers and stone from the besieged palace. Indeed, the site occupied by 'Drinks 2 Drink' has been used to supply food and wine continuously since 1617.

Passing the 'floral walls' of Red Lion Street, near the top of the High Street hangs the recently renovated original town clock, made and first installed by James Padbury, who died in 1898, the last of a family of local clockmakers.

At the very top of the High Street you will be able to spot St Peter's Street, considered by many to be the prettiest street in Hampshire and home to the Bunch of Grapes. This

The High Street looking towards St George's Square. (T3664M)

The jubilee clock in St George's Square. (T3664A)

16th-century inn, which features in many good beer guides, prides itself on being a traditional country pub with beer still served straight from the barrel with an upright piano for entertainment. No jukebox has ever gained entry here! The 'Grapes' has been in the hands of the Pink family for five generations, with the present landlord hopeful that one of his daughters will continue the tradition.

Since 720 there has been a church in the town. However, the first – along with the rest of the town – was destroyed by the Danes. Luckily the Saxon font was found in 1933 in nearby Houchin Street and can be seen in St Peter's Church today.

Within easy walking distance of the town centre are a number of nature reserves. One example is The Moors, a fascinating wetland area to the south of the town, nationally important for its botanical and invertebrate communities and where springs feed the Hamble.

Acid-loving plants such as heath-spotted orchids and cross-leaved heath can be found growing alongside species that prefer chalky soils, like cowslips and milkwort. A number of scarce snails make their home in The Moors, including the

nationally-protected Desmoulin's Whorl – otherwise known as the Newbury Bypass snail!

The mill pond of The Moors once powered Waltham Chase Mill, which was mentioned in the Domesday Book. The surviving building is largely Victorian and a unique twin pitchback watermill. It was the subject of a BBC TV series called *Salvage Squad* in January 2003, when a team helped rebuild the waterwheel. The mill is open to the public on National Heritage Day each September, when flour is milled and offered for sale.

Bishop's Waltham has won a number of awards, including first prize in the Small Town and Best Kept Village categories in the Southern England in Bloom 1998 competition. In 2004, for the first time, a Hidden Gardens event saw 12 very different gardens open to the public.

Offering modern day essentials with a wealth of old-world charm, Bishop's Waltham has a host of attractions for both visitor and resident alike. Its wide range of specialist shops and eating establishments is complemented by fascinating historical and natural features meandering out from a floral-lined award-winning centre.

A Town Trail leaflet is available from tourist information centres, giving further information on places of interest and suggested further reading.

Botley's bloody beginnings

BENEATH BOTLEY'S pleasant and unassuming facade lies a colourful and sometimes violent history. The village, whose small hub – congenial shops, cafés and pubs – is familiar to many motorists as they pass along the busy A334, once played host to a cruel murder.

Behind Botley's pleasant facade lies a tale of some turmoil.

On 4 March 1800, Private John Diggon went to the gallows for beating and killing a 70-year-old peddlar from Swanmore called

The Old Forge in Botley High Street, on the left, looking towards the village centre, with Botley House on the right. (T4265Q)

All Saints' Church.
(T4265M)

Thomas Webb as he was walking home from the village after buying eggs. Webb was found covered in blood and dirt with the broken stump of an army bayonet lodged in his neck.

The culprit, Diggon, was a soldier in the Tarbert Fencibles, King George III's regiment, camped near Botley to defend against a possible French invasion. It is said his body hung in chains near the site of the murder for up to 40 years before being buried! A memorial to the bloody deed is still to be seen at the entrance to the village's railway station.

In the general election of December 1885, a mob from Hedge End and Bursledon stormed into the village and smashed the windows of most of the properties in the High Street and taunted and abused villagers. Officials and two policemen had to barricade themselves into the polling station – then the village primary school, now homes – to prevent the removal of the ballot box. Several men were later sent to prison for lawlessness. Village History Society archivist, Dennis Stokes, a Botley resident for 40 years, says it is still not clear why this happened. He believes it may have been rivalry between the two villages, each thinking that they had more 'class'. Another theory is that election

Botley Mills, which date to around 1770. Today they have a new lease of life as several businesses and retailers have their headquarters there. Late in 2004 The Naked Baker opened on the site, bringing history full circle. (T4265H)

time was an excuse for men to get drunk and high spirited. Either way, he would be happy to hear of any other possible explanations.

Another political animal who once lived in Botley was 19th-century writer and activist William Cobbett (1763–1835). Cobbett was a great thorn in the side of the Government of the day and was a champion of the cause of the rural worker against the changes wrought by the Industrial Revolution. He also started the radical weekly newsletter, the *Political Register*. His legacy today lies in his former house opposite the water on the outskirts of the village. His name also adorns one of the bars of the popular Bugle Inn – one of Botley's watering holes.

Today, the village, which has

The Old Gatehouse, Botley – a replacement for the earlier toll house demolished during the building of the Bishopstoke to Gosport railway in the 1840s. The toll house was part of the Lower St Cross, Mill Lane and Park Gate Turnpike of 1810. (T4265FF)

Roman origins, is better known for its community spirit, which brings people together, than its uprisings. There is an active twinning association, which organises regular social events with the village's French counterpart, St Jean Brevalay in Brittany, and an active parish council that takes great pride in the village and its future.

More has been developed for young people, who make up a large proportion of the 5,000 or so population, with a new youth centre and recreation ground in western Botley.

2004 saw the first day-long Botley festival in the village, at which 6,000 visitors helped raise more than £1,600 for Botley First Responders. The 2005 summer extravaganza aims to hit the £5,000 mark. Proceeds will go towards an extension to Botley's pretty All Saints' Church, built in 1836, to provide new community facilities. Other fund-raising activities and grant applications have also led to the makeover of the village's most striking building, the Market Hall. The neo-classical building dating from 1848, commissioned by then Lord of the Manor, James Warner, and once used by trading farmers, is today used by the playgroups, badminton club and mother and toddler groups, but it is hoped that a new acoustic ceiling and sound system will mean the hall can reach its full potential and stage shows and musical performances. Whether as a visitor you decide to sample Botley's interesting shops, drop into the former mill (which it is hoped will one day be a museum) or wander near the Hamble up to nearby Manor Farm, evidence of Botley's fascinating past is never far away.

Bountiful Broughton

IT'S A LONG, long way to Broughton, or so it seems. And it doesn't matter which approach you choose, the village feels remote, inaccessible, cut off... Perhaps that's why it is such a self-contained, independent-spirited village – even by the locals' own admission.

Broughton is eye candy: a hotchpotch of the best of vernacular styles

To Stockbridge and beyond in search of Broughton, a beautiful village with a feisty spirit.

– traditional thatch that sweeps so low it nearly brushes the ground, Georgian elegance, Victorian cottages and characterful contemporary

'The Thatch' in the High Street. (F3515A)

Broughton well in the
High Street was sunk
in the drought of 1921.
It stands as a
memorial to Lt John
Fripp, killed in action
in October 1915.
(F3515J)

buildings. It's a higgledy-piggledy mix and yet nothing looks out of place, not even the topiary hedges.

Broughton is centred around its church, two pubs, a village store and post office and, on one side, the Wallop Brook wandering along on its way to the River Test. This is a village that has won Southern England in Bloom nine times, as well as the coveted Hampshire Best Kept Village award.

Inevitably, the village draws visitors. Some are walkers. There are, apparently, 20 footpaths in the area as well as Broughton Down nature reserve – rich chalk grassland with cowslips, rock roses and orchids smothered by butterflies in summer.

Others are attracted by the sights, such as the historic circular dovecote in the churchyard (with 482 nesting boxes in the thickness of its walls) built in 1684 on the site of a previous one that dated from 1340.

Art enthusiasts can discover the Clarendon Way's entrance and exit from the village, both marked by contemporary artwork commissioned, along with an imaginative new village sign on the old pound, as a permanent commemoration of the Millennium.

Or there's The Garden Gallery,

The circular dovecote in the churchyard has 482 nesting sites. It was built in 1684 on the site of a previous one dating from 1340. (F3515D)

A view of Broughton
House from the
churchyard. (F3515E)

The ford across Wallop
Brook at the end of
Dixons Lane.
(F3515L)

created by garden designer Rachel Bebb, which celebrated its 10th anniversary of promoting works of art for gardens (including sculpture, pots and furniture) by holding a special exhibition of works in stone, bronze, marble and glass.

Pam Dawkins, Broughton born and bred, recalls a very different village in her childhood. 'When I was young there were 14 shops, whereas now we have just the one, and the village was made up of agricultural workers. But changes have brought in people with skills we didn't have here before, so the sense of community is still here, it's just a little different.'

Lynda Boulton, also born in Broughton and now clerk to the parish council and farmer's wife, living in one of the last farms still within the village, agrees: 'Because Broughton is some distance from other towns we've developed an infrastructure that has given villagers a strong sense of community and place.

'Also, we've always looked to the future and tried to retain a balance because what makes this community is the mix. We've absorbed people who have moved in, but we've also been determined to keep our young-sters.

'We've retained our village school and we were one of the first villages to have affordable housing, a scheme pushed through by the parish council when we recognised how fast house prices were rising.'

This is indeed a village that likes to be in control of its own destiny – to the extent that it has established, with Mottisfont, its own bus service, run by volunteers, to meet the needs of the community.

'It was held up by Hampshire County Council as a prime example of its kind. In fact they wanted to take it over, but we said, "no thank you,"' Lynda adds, rather firmly.

The former Methodist church in the High Street, which is now a private residence. (F3515K)

Typically English – a beautifully picturesque cottage in Rookery Lane. (F3515B)

Not that anyone needs to go far. The village has its own doctor's surgery and, in terms of leisure activities, there's always something going on: the church fêtes, school fêtes, the May fête, open gardens, the flower show and Christmas market to mention a very few. At the last count there were 20-plus clubs and organisations.

'There's always lots going on,' said Pam. 'In fact there's such a tremendous amount it's quite staggering; if you can't find what you want to do, villagers will support you in setting something up!'

Lynda added: 'Last year, we built a skate park and that was driven by the over-11s and their parents.'

'It's the sort of place where, if you need help, people rally round,' enthuses Bob Gillespie, who runs the village store and post office with his partner, Judith Martins. Their lives were changed for ever by a dinner party in the next village, where they heard that the village store and post office in Broughton was for sale. 'Next thing I knew, we were committed to taking it over!' remembers Bob. It has meant a complete change of lifestyle for the pair of them, but five years on the business is thriving, thanks to the terrific support of villagers.

It does seem to be that sort of place. Organisations work together for big fund-raising events and when anyone is ill, they get support in a quiet, tactful, gentle way.

'Maybe,' suggests Lynda, 'villages give people the opportunity to open their hearts.'

Captivating Candovers

Discover the Candover Valley's lush pastureland, old footpaths and buried church.

NAMED AFTER the stream that runs through this wide, park-like valley, Brown Candover, Chilton Candover and Preston Candover are a trio of rather elegant little villages, banded together under the collective title The Candovers, but with quite separate identities.

Travelling north from Alresford on the B3046, Brown Candover is the first of the three and quietly impressive, with a delightful view uphill to the picturesque church of St Peter's. Situated a field away from the road and beyond the cricket pitch, the church and adjacent village hall make an idyllic backdrop to a country cricket match.

The church, built in 1845, is typically rural Hampshire, all flint and stone. Next door the hall is as

Once a centre of activity; the village pump with the spire of St Mary the Virgin Church behind. (J3962E)

pretty as a club pavilion could be with a verandah and steps down to a terrace. Activities here include whist, bingo and keep-fit. Annual events on the field in front feature the summer fête and village barbecue.

Preston Candover's church, St Mary the Virgin, rises majestically from the landscape. (J3962C)

Close by, the Wayfarers' Walk passes through the village before crossing the Oxdrove – a path once used to drive cattle from South Wales to markets in Surrey and Kent. This way runs along the valley beside The Candovers and has given its name to the valley benefice magazine.

The middle settlement, Chilton Candover, is the intriguing home to a couple of surprises: a buried church and what is believed to be, at nearly half-a-mile long, the longest avenue of yews in England. The village is also a very good example of Elizabethan depopulation. Perhaps it is the air of abandonment that gives the settlement its haunting and romantic atmosphere. The avenue of yews leads nowhere (it is thought there was a manor house at the head of the avenue, immediately west of the church, which was destroyed in the 18th century), and the buried church of St Nicholas is actually a partially sunken Norman crypt.

This is all that remains of an ancient church, built in about 1100. A later church was built on the same site in the 14th century but demolished in 1878 and entirely forgotten, except by one old man who remembered, when he was a boy, going under the church into a big hole and kicking skulls around! His recollections prompted the then rector to excavate the site in 1927. Today it is still an enjoyable discovery, found in the middle of a small stone wall-enclosed graveyard up the valley slope.

The field surrounding the church is uneven, full of mounds and hollows and the uncertain outlines of ridges and platforms that are all that is left of the mediaeval village, which was demolished in 1562 when the population was dispersed and the land enclosed for grazing sheep. Even today there is only a mere scattering of cottages with one or two more substantial farmhouses.

Preston Candover, set among towering beech and horse chestnut trees, is the largest of the three and a slightly unlikely mix of dairy herds and tennis club, allotments and skate ramp. It feels both grand and comfortable, smart and rural by turn. There's a popular primary school, shop and post office, village hall, an inn and, opposite, the Victorian church of St Mary's with its slender, elegant spire. In the undisturbed quiet of a Saturday afternoon there's a feeling of little happening very slowly.

'It may look quiet, but it's frenetic

This yew avenue at Chilton Candover is believed to be the longest in the country. (J3962G)

when you live here,' the Revd David Keighley assures us – hardly surprising when he has responsibility for four parishes encompassing five churches. 'We're very fortunate as there's a tradition of involvement with the church in rural parishes,' David continues. 'People move into a village and want to get involved.'

There are certainly plenty of opportunities for involvement, with choirs, bands, bellringing, discussion groups and a wide range of services including traditional, all-age (babies to grandparents), pet (hamsters to horses) and meditative services.

Graze elegy… cattle chew the cud in Preston Candover. (J3962B)

Peaceful presence… just one of many lovely old cottages in Preston Candover. (J3962F)

Some, like the Taizé service (a quiet, meditative service lit by candles and accompanied by cello and flute music) attract visitors from far afield.

Annual events are also a curious combination of nativity plays and

duck races, harvest suppers and a Good Friday pilgrimage down the valley to all five churches with a picnic on the way.

It is, overall, family-orientated. The public house, the Purefoy Arms, is a family concern run by mum, dad, two daughters and one son-in-law and offers a real country local with quiz nights, curry nights and a barbecue with a bouncy castle on bank holidays. Along the road, in the village hall, there's a toddler group, twice-weekly doctor's surgery, square dancing, yoga, a gardening club and drama groups.

'There's an enormous amount going on,' David says. 'Many choose to live in villages for the purpose of getting involved in the family atmosphere of a rural community.' And with its fireworks display, barn dance (barn kindly supplied by local family, the Sainsburys), over-60s dinners and, less obviously, unobtrusive support for villagers in need, The Candovers are united in being a very caring cluster of villages.

Dream of escape

WHEN CITY dwellers fantasise about living in a village in the country, they dream of Cheriton. They may not know it, but they do. For Cheriton has everything the quintessential English village should possess: a bubbling brook, a thriving cricket team, a quaint family-run pub, a bustling village store… and it is immeasurably picturesque.

Even the approach to Cheriton is enjoyable: either through a verdant

Strolling through picture book-lovely Cheriton

tunnel of green from Alresford, or along the A272, a prosaic name for a road which takes you up into the sky where, with the horizon, on every side the chalk downs and tree-flanked fields of Hampshire roll away effortlessly.

Cheriton is the birthplace and playground of the River Itchen, which, criss-crossed by low, 'Pooh-sticks' bridges, winds and gurgles its way through the village green and past houses washed in pink, cream and white under thatch and wavy, tiled roofs.

Ducks waddle and paddle on its banks and children play on bikes and skateboards. Down one lane is Cheriton primary school, housed in the sort of traditional Victorian school building you usually see in picture books (partly because many village schools have long been converted into homes). And, tucked

The 12th-century church of St Michael and All Angels. (T3379B)

into the heart of the village, lying languidly on what is believed to be a prehistoric burial mound or long barrow, is the 12th-century church of St Michael and All Angels.

Underlying everything is a sense of continual activity and busyness. For this is a community kept buoyant by those who have moved into the area working alongside those whose families have been here for generations.

The village store had closed until current owners, Martin and Sandy Hubbard, moved in. Five-and-a-half years later it is a thriving business, offering shoe repairs, dry cleaning, video rental, photography development, fresh fruit and vegetables, wine and daily deliveries from a local bakery. Indeed, Sandy and Martin actively source local suppliers. Most importantly it offers a service that is beyond price – an informal place for villagers to chat. It appears that only the socially active live here as there's a thriving cricket team, Scouts, yoga in the village hall, bell-ringing and a church choir, as well as the popular Cheriton Players, who stage three sell-out productions annually.

Probably, however, Cheriton is best known for the rather quaint, if

The River Itchen wandering through the village gives it a peaceful air. (T3379N)

Ducks forage on the village green. (T3379M)

This picturesque bridge crosses the River Itchen. (T3379J)

not idiosyncratic, Flower Pots Inn. The rather robust red-brick exterior gives little away… but inside, like Cheriton itself, its everything you want from an unspoilt village pub.

The family owners (with mum as landlord) have taken all our favourite memories and expectations of a proper local and thrown them in the mix. They brew their own award-winning beers (Cheriton Brewhouse is just across the pub car park) served

from casks behind the bar. One bar area is like a comfortable sitting room with armchairs and stripy wallpaper, while the other has a huge open fire in winter. Daughter Jo is responsible for food (serving up big helpings of hot pot and colossal steak baps) and on Wednesday it's curry night with real Punjabi cuisine. (A country local with proper curry – how perfect can it get?) Every August bank holiday the hordes descend for the Pots' increasingly popular beer festival. Overall, Cheriton is a success story because the villagers put so much effort into making their community work.

And, like the very individual Flower Pots Inn, Cheriton is an eclectic mix of the very best of contemporary country life... and it works.

This 17th-century cottage at North End, Cheriton, sports a surprising variety of roofing materials. (T3379F)

This road used to lead to Freeman's wood yard. (T3379L)

Chocolate-box Chilbolton

Teeming with thatched cottages, beside the River Test, Chilbolton is one of Hampshire's prettiest villages.

BEAUTIFUL thatched cottages stand sentinel along the old route into the village, giving a chocolate-box feel to picturesque Chilbolton. In fact, it's the sheer number of these quaint buildings which first strikes the visitor.

It's an impressive picture now, but signs are that the first residents arrived long before these now-listed buildings, which give Chilbolton its special character. Archaeologists have found several flints and axe heads dating from the Stone Age, along with Roman coins.

The village church, St Mary the

This bridge once formed part of the Sprat and Winkle line. (J3890M)

Fullerton Mill commands the river. (J3890Q)

This thatched cottage has been extended since its more humble origins. (J3890G)

Less, is over 700 years old. Its name is a riddle. It is thought that a larger church was dedicated to St Mary in Andover in the 14th century, so the smaller one at Chilbolton adopted 'Less' into its title.

St Mary the Less nearly went up in flames in 1811 after fire destroyed a quarter of the village. *Chilbolton Fragments*, a book produced by resident Eleanor Lockyer, recalls the blaze at 2am one June morning when flames, which began at the home of Robert Cole, a farmer, swept through 13 homes, eight barns, six stables, five granaries, several cart houses and their contents. The church was threatened, but firemen from Andover and Stockbridge managed to keep it safe.

The book reveals that Chilbolton also had a brewery during Victorian times, though ale production ceased in dramatic circumstances.

In January 1884, a young maltster called Smith was working at the building, which was owned by the Tilbury family. For some reason, the brewery exploded, damaging the structure beyond repair.

Miraculously, Smith cheated death, the blast blowing him clear of the wreckage. His co-workers found him lying in a nearby field, having been thrown around 30 yards.

Today, Chilbolton is famed for its distinctive observatory, visible for miles around. It opened in April 1967, beside the old airfield, which was home to US servicemen in World

The village church of St Mary the Less. (J3890D)

War Two. The observatory had its teething troubles as, just a few months into service, it began screeching when rotating. The problem was a bearing that was sinking into the ground. To replace it, engineers lifted the entire structure, some 400 tons, off the ground with hydraulic jacks. In the

The Mayfly pub with the Test running past. (J3890R)

years since, the observatory has provided weather data and satellite communications.

The village itself is home to around 1,000 people. Annette Keys has watched it evolve since moving to the village in 1963. 'There's been a lot of development in the last 50 years, but the core of the village is still the same,' she said.

A conservation area covers the heart of Chilbolton. It has even retained its traditional red telephone boxes, after residents lobbied BT against installing modern ones.

Chilbolton is traditional, yes, but it is not trapped in a time bubble. The busy village hall is home to a range of events, from amateur dramatics to badminton and from weddings to martial arts.

There is also the village pub, the Abbot's Mitre, which stands opposite Chilbolton Stores and post office. Shop owners Richard and Carol Hay came to the village in 2004. The husband-and-wife team modernised the store to secure the long-term future of the business. And, judging by the flow of customers, a pleasing bustle increasingly rare elsewhere still exists in Chilbolton.

Indeed, a short walk through this picturesque retreat would leave few people in doubt about why this corner of Hampshire is so popular.

A cottage alongside the River Meon at Corhampton. (T3596A)

Fusion confusion

Two into one does go for Corhampton and Meonstoke, but it hasn't been without its problems.

IT WAS in 1927 that Corhampton and Meonstoke, previously two villages, were fused into one parish. It is now sketchy where the border lies and some residents disagree with the powers that be. Royal Mail, Winchester City Council and most mapmakers put Corhampton north of Meonstoke. Many inhabitants take the River Meon as the border, which puts Corhampton on the western bank and Meonstoke on the east.

The first settlers arrived over 2,000 years ago. Roman remains were found east of Meonstoke, and a gable from an excavated building is now at the British Museum. The present parish grew up on the junction of two roads, which meet where the River Meon cuts through the South Downs.

St Andrew's Church at Meonstoke. (T3596F)

Corhampton was owned by a long line of wealthy families, while Meonstoke was a possession of the Crown and then the Church. In the 14th century, Meonstoke came under the control of William of Wykeham, founder of Winchester College. The oldest surviving building in the parish is the Grade I listed Corhampton Saxon Church, built in 1020.

Chris Maxse has lived in Meonstoke for 35 years and conducts walking tours around Winchester. Turning his hand to his home parish,

Hillside Cottages in the
High Street at
Meonstoke. (T3596J)

he is in no doubt as to the building's significance. 'It's one of the most important small Saxon churches in the land.'

The building is complete, apart from the eastern end, which collapsed when a nearby road was widened in 1842. Inside is a fine Saxon chancel arch, an altar, and a collection of wall paintings. Mr Maxse recalls that, in 2002, the church welcomed the then Archbishop of Canterbury, George Carey, who was amazed to find it was older than Canterbury Cathedral. One part of the church is believed to date from before 1020. Set into the southern wall outside the main entrance is a sundial, thought to be from the time of King Alfred the Great.

A few paces from the sundial is a yew tree, reckoned to be one of the oldest in Hampshire. 'There's only one way to find out how old it is, and that would be to cut it down, but that would be a pity,' says Mr Maxse.

St Andrew's Church in Meonstoke, which is Grade II listed, was built in 1230. Larger than its Saxon counterpart, it is recognisable by its square wooden tower, built in 1905. The interior has changed little over eight centuries, although the roof at the eastern end was covered in plaster during the Georgian era. It was nearly a fatal decision, as the roof

Roger and Mary Morfill outside the village stores. (T3596E)

caved in during a service in the Victorian period and the falling plaster missed the then rector, Charles Hume, by inches.

The Meon Hall, built in 1982, stands on the eastern edge of Meonstoke and boasts two sizeable rooms and adjoining playing fields. Mr Maxse says it is a great improvement on the former village hall, which was an 'old tin hut'.

Meonstoke's High Street boasts a picturesque collection of homes, most dating from shortly after 1719. In that year, a fire gutted most of the buildings in the street. Many cottages bear the names of the shops and pubs they used to house before being

The interior of the Grade I-listed Corhampton Saxon church. (T3596CJ)

converted into private homes. Meonstoke also still has one pub – The Buck's Head – beside the river. Residents also argue that they have a village store and post office, but again, the boundary is hazy.

Sub-postmaster Roger Morfill says he lives in Meonstoke, but his employer disagrees. 'According to my contract, I'm working in "Meonstoke Post Office", but the postal address is "Corhampton".'

He says the parish is '12 miles from everywhere', being a near equal distance from Winchester, Southampton, Portsmouth, Petersfield and Alton. 'We're in the middle of nothing, it's great.' Mr Morfill has run the stores for nine years with his wife, Mary, who is a deacon at a church in nearby Swanmore.

Walking around the parish, it is certainly difficult to spot where Meonstoke begins and Corhampton ends, especially as the dividing river splits into two channels.

Then again, as both villages have no shortage of picture postcard views, to the casual visitor it hardly matters where the boundary lies. Perhaps the mapmakers can be forgiven after all!

Far from the madding crowd. (T3596DJ)

Delightful Droxford

Stretched along the busy A32, the best of Droxford is hidden from view.

DROXFORD carries its past quietly. For here, among this elegant cluster of predominantly Georgian houses, gathered around a triangular village square, history was made.

In fact Droxford has a few claims to fame, one culinary (this was where the Jerusalem artichoke first flourished in the UK), one sporting (Izaak Walton, author of *The Compleat Angler*, fished the Meon here) and one of worldwide significance. For it was at Droxford that Churchill decided the timing of the Allied invasion of Europe. The

The normally busy A32 winds its way through the Meon valley village of Droxford. (T3998T)

village was suggested by the station-master at Southampton, when he was asked where in his area a train could stand unobtrusively for some days within the protection of a cutting. And so Droxford station became, in June 1944, D-day headquarters for the members of the Allied Expeditionary Force: among them not only Churchill, but also Eisenhower, de Gaulle, Eden and Bevin.

Today, Droxford is as hidden as its past. Rush through on the A32 and you'll miss it. You need to stroll down the lanes and footpaths to discover its sudden solitude.

This is where the chalk downs dip into rich clay – hence there's less thatch and more brick and tile – although the lovely local red-grey brick is often painted over in washes of white and cream.

From the village square the Wayfarers' Way wanders past the village hall (once the old school and still used by the new school for the summer play) and handsome Old Rectory (glimpsed behind high, old walls and railings) to the churchyard abutting the Meon's lush water-meadows. Well-hidden from the main road, this is an idyllic and secluded spot for the church, St Mary and All Saints, which boasts features from all the architectural periods from Norman through Tudor and

This bridge at Droxford carries the Wayfarers' Way over the River Meon. (T39998G)

Jacobean to Georgian and Victorian. What sets it apart, however, are dormer windows, which introduce a quaint touch of domesticity, and an unusual stair-turret thought to be unique in the county.

It appears to be the quintessential village church, untouched by the passing of time, but the new rector is ensuring that Droxford has a broad church. 'In a village, a church has to be all things to all people,' explains the Revd Jim Foley, who is introducing child-friendly elements such as a youth orchestra and holiday club. 'On some days there are as many as five services, and on the first Sunday of the month we hold a 1662 prayer book service at 8.30am followed by a family service with Power Point presentation, coffee and muffins,

musicians and video clips. So, we go from St James to modern times in the course of one hour… and it works!

'There's an awful lot going on in Droxford,' he continues: 'There are so many different clubs and activities you can go out and do something every night and every day. There really is a strong sense of community and a good cross-section of people.' He's particularly proud of what he describes as 'the strong sense of people caring for each other' – examples of this are the community bus and the hospital driver service.

But the community has changed quite dramatically over the lifetimes of the locals. Increasingly, villages like Droxford attract commuters. Once the village was nicknamed HMS *Droxford*, as there were lots of

Climbers around the porch give a rural feel to this cottage alongside the busy A32. (T3998B)

young naval officers living here after the war. Then IBM took over and now it's gone from HMS to NHS Droxford as many young doctors have moved in. But the Manor House and the Old Rectory have had families in them for generations – so there's a good mix of new and old.

One villager, Jean Newman, recalls how times have changed: 'I remember how, at one time, everybody knew everyone else in the village, but many people were related to each other so you had to be careful what you said!

'There used to be more village occasions, too, but we still have the summer fête and the summer barbecue and a lot of people come to that.

'When I was younger there were about 13 shops, but they were gradually closed down and became houses. I'm pleased we have the post office (attached to one of the village pubs, the Baker's Arms) and there's a garage shop now, too, but the produce market at the village hall is very popular. Villagers, especially the more elderly, need these facilities and it is nice to have somewhere to meet people and have a natter. From Easter to September there are teas on Saturdays and Sundays in the village hall too.' Droxford's facilities also include a police station and doctor's surgery.

The produce market every Friday afternoon in the village hall has been particularly successful. Locals bring home-grown vegetables and fruit, hand-made cards and cushions to sell and villagers can come in and enjoy afternoon tea with homemade cakes. This popular market has been running for just two years and has become an important facet of village life.

But even though Droxford may have changed, Jean feels very lucky to live there: 'I would never leave. We have some of the most beautiful views and there are lovely walks along the old railway line, up on the downs past the school or down by the river, it really is a lovely place...'

The Wayfarers' Way passes along an avenue of trees planted in 1962 by Edward Attrill. (T3998E)

Fête better than debt

DESPITE a rapid rise in house prices, which has made it difficult for many of the long-standing village families to stay, East Meon retains a strong sense of community. In a spot which has its fair share of properties empty for the five days between weekends, explains villager Denys Rider, it's the residents who still make East Meon what it is.

Denys has lived in the parish since 1953, was educated at former Westbury House Preparatory School nearby, and helps compile the newsletter, *Meon Matters*. 'It's about participation,' says retired farmer Denys, now 72. 'You don't have entertainment provided like you do in the town. Here we make our own entertainment.'

One highlight of the calendar in this pretty village on the tip of the Meon Valley is the May Fête, held on a bank holiday weekend to raise funds for the village hall. Built in the 1970s, the hall is still very much at the hub of the community. The event, which attracts up to 4,000 visitors a year, makes thousands of pounds for the hall and is a genuine country fair. As such, it has dog, tractor and sheep shows and traditional games such as 'bowling for the pig'.

East Meon, though part empty much of the week, still has a sense of community.

Villagers also take great pride in their beautifully tended gardens, and have opened them to the public annually for 20 years. East Meon's Garden Club has raised £26,000 for worthy local causes from this colourful corner of rural England.

A sense of community spirit has been evident in East Meon through the centuries. For example, there are five almshouses, built in 1863, in front of the striking Norman church, All Saints', established for the needy in the parish. The cottages are still occupied today by the less fortunate and the elderly.

The river takes pride of place outside these cottages and the Izaak Walton pub in the High Street. (J3739D)

This flint bridge crosses the River Meon in the High Street. (J3739L)

Ye Olde George Inn, in Church Street, is one of two pubs in the village, which also boasts a shop and a school. (J3739H)

Norman church All Saints' with the village laid out below it. (J3739G)

If 'city types' are attracted to East Meon today, it was farmers who formed the community 100 years ago. And, interestingly, it's the names of those local farmers which give clue to their origins – Atkinson, Mason and Wren, all very familiar in their native Cumbria, are now the family names in East Meon, explains Denys. Their forebears began to make the journey southward at the beginning of the 20th century, attracted by the cheap rents.

Much of the farmland in the parish was then owned by Lord and Lady Peel (relatives of the father of the police force, Sir Robert Peel), who moved to East Meon at the end of the 19th century and built the huge, stately home called Leydene in the south of the parish.

The house was taken over at the outbreak of World War Two by the Royal Navy, because of its location looking towards Portsmouth, and turned into HMS *Mercury* – a signal station – and was only closed as such two years ago. Today, it is 'Leydene House', a complex of luxury flats.

Indeed, wartime was an eventful time for the village, which then as now had a population of around 1,000, not least when a German bomber squadron dropped all their

incendiary bombs on nearby Westbury Forest, leaving it blazing through the night. It is believed that the Germans were on a mission to attack the Meon Valley railway when they were caught by British planes and released their weapons to lose weight to make a speedy retreat.

Denys recalls seeing the fire ripping through the woods from his window at school. 'The next day we went up to the woods and started looking for unexploded bombs.'

Like West Meon down the road, East Meon, nestling snugly alongside the river, has many delights to uncover and a wealth of history in which to immerse oneself. And there's no better way to find out more about this Hampshire village than to simply take a look around – preferably at a leisurely pace!

Far from the madding crowd

EASTON VILLAGE is as leisurely as a Sunday afternoon. Nestled alongside the River Itchen, it feels a very long way from the madding crowd, yet it is less than a 10-minute drive from the bustle of Winchester.

This small village boasts two pubs and an international reputation and is well worth exploring.

It's equally astonishing to discover that this unassuming little village, with its relaxed bonhomie and quaint cluster of thatch and flint-knapped homes, has an international reputation. For the Itchen, considered the best chalk-stream in the country, if not the world, has attracted anglers from around the globe, including celebrities, politic-

ians and notables such as Eric Clapton and Jimmy Carter, the late Roy Jenkins and the director of New York's Museum of Modern Art.

'Easton is almost the perfect village, although I might be biased,' says George Burnand, who has lived on the edge of the village most of his life and now runs Strutt & Parker estate agents in Winchester. He continues: 'Apart from not having a shop it has everything else you might expect and, with the likes of the up-and-coming Judes Ice, perhaps a little bit more!'

Easton is as spread out as a small village can be, with the appealing Norman church, with its distinctive horseshoe-arched doorway, in one direction and the village hall and cricket ground in another.

The Cricketers Inn, the quintessential locals' pub, is at the centre of the village, both geographically and socially. In a venture that typifies

Can a village get more peaceful than this? (T3375A)

Easton's strong sense of community, a trio of villagers bought the inn last December, so it really is run by the village for the village.

Perhaps this explains its com-fortable home-from-home ambi-ance. Here all-comers can enjoy quiz nights, get-togethers for big matches on the big screen, games of giant Jenga, live jazz on Wednesdays and

St Mary's nestles in the trees above the River Itchen. (T3375R)

hearty helpings of home-cooked, traditional pub food.

Unusually for a village this size, Easton supports two pubs, as there is also the Chestnut Horse on the road towards Avington. You'll get a warm welcome here, too, but otherwise this is a very different establishment, having achieved a county-wide reputation for its food.

Recognition has arrived in the form of a food award in the latest edition of *The Good Pub Guide*. This 16th-century pub, despite its resident ghost, is invitingly snug with cosy furnishings in scarlet and olive, piles of squashy cushions, pictures on every spare space of wall and tankards marching across the beamed ceilings.

A handful of locals enjoying a lunchtime drink assured me that in the summer the terrace (unexpectedly Mediterranean in style, with terracotta-coloured walls, wicker hanging baskets and patio heaters) is a riot of floral colour.

The Chestnut Horse has just started serving cream teas during the afternoon to tempt hikers and strollers. For this place of riverbank, woods and meadows is walking country. Both the Pilgrims' Way (Winchester to Canterbury) and the Itchen Way pass through the village, and there are regular rogation walks and WI walks (non-members and men welcome) – the latter sensibly usually ending up at a pub for lunch. Discover a copy of the *Easton & Martyr Worthy News* for further information.

So, Easton is full of unexpected delights and the most unexpected and the most delightful is the easy friendliness extended by the locals to visitors. A 10-minute chat and you feel that you're part of the community and looking forward to the village fête on August bank holiday and the Christmas pantomime (apparently good enough to rival any professional production).

'I remember bicycling down to watch my father play cricket and have even had a few games myself,' says George Burnand. 'I always try to make it back to the pantomime, which while my own acting prowess has never been up to it, three members of the family have made appearances and my father is a regular!'

You're also initiated into the village tit-bits and discover that this was comedian Jack Dee's childhood home – which perhaps explains his nonchalant and ever so slightly out-of-kilter sense of humour, very much in keeping with Easton's take on life.

'The village has changed over the years but has always managed to retain a good atmosphere with a mix of people, from those who were born in the village to some who have recently moved in,' says George . 'It is a village where it is difficult not to get involved one way or other.'

Hiltingbury highlights

I F Chandler's Ford is a lovely place to live, Hiltingbury, to many, is even better. Some would have it that the area of wooded high ground on the northern end of the village is 'the posh end' of Chandler's Ford. Its tree-lined residential roads are characterised by large houses and bungalows, many with generously sized gardens.

Attractions include lakes that once formed part of an Edwardian garden and a meadow which is a haven for butterflies. The affluence of Hiltingbury is underlined by the success of its secondary school, Thornden, which is never far from the top of the Hampshire league table for GCSE results and by its voting habits. In borough council elections, it is solidly Conservative.

Much of the area remained woods or heath until the 1950s, and developers are now busy filling in any surviving green gaps, which seems to include many of the bigger back

Discover the delights of Hiltingbury with its tree-lined streets, and turn off the beaten track to discover some of the wildlife.

Treescape in the woods around Hiltingbury Lake. (T4299N)

gardens. Some houses have been replaced by blocks of flats, and councillors are fighting to prevent the dwindling supply of bungalows being replaced by two-storey houses.

The church of St Martin in the Wood... in the wood. (T4299R)

Hocombe Mead Nature Reserve on the edge of Hiltingbury. (T4299T)

The most impressive street for a stroll is Lakewood Road, which has some of the grandest homes, many of the biggest gardens and some of the tallest oaks. Merdon Avenue and parts of Kingsway have also kept a Hiltingbury flavour. Hiltingbury was originally far more grand than it is now and, occasionally, you can glimpse an older house of mansion-like proportions, now hemmed in by more recent additions. Hiltingbury Lakes, now a public park, is a remnant of the garden of one of the early mansions, the since-demol-

Feeding the ducks on Hiltingbury Lake, which was originally part of an Edwardian water garden. (T4299K)

ished Merdon House. It is, however, still a good spot for a picnic.

The six lakes, of varying sizes and totalling two acres, were created by damming a stream. The upper one is by far the largest but some of the lower ones retain more of the feel of an Edwardian water garden. Mallard and moorhen nest on an island in the big lake and there are grey wagtail, too. Less well known, however, is Hiltingbury's other haven for wildlife.

Hocombe Mead is home to nearly 30 species of butterfly and a host of rare plants. It's a long, thin site, along the valley of a stream between Hocombe Road and Hiltingbury Road near Hursley Road, with parking provision for visitors at the Ashdown Drive end of Ashdown Road. Paths offer a circular route, taking in meadow and coppiced woodland that is 400 years old. And on the western edge of Hiltingbury, across Hursley Road, there's a woodland walk from Ramalley Lane to Valley Park, crossing the single track Romsey railway.

Unique Houghton

DATING back to the Stone Age, the village of Houghton, on the banks of the River Test, has survived invasions from the Romans and the Normans but has retained its unique character. Just three miles away from Stock-

The war memorial sits in the heart of the village, opposite the Boot Inn. (J4321B)

Houghton – a picturesque beauty spot.

bridge, the Houghton familiar to all today started to take shape after the Roman occupation but has more in

*The picturesque village
is alive with gorgeous
chocolate-box cottages.
(J4321D)*

common with its Saxon forebears, who settled the winding river banks. With the arrival of William the Conqueror came the Domesday survey and this showed that there was a large manor in the village called Houghton Drayton and four smaller estates. The survey also revealed that the manor was held by the Bishop of Winchester and valued at £30.

The village follows the line of the Test. The candlestick chimney stacks seem to stand sentinel over the waters. (J4321G)

The meandering Test. (J4321F)

Much later on, in 1637, the poor of the village benefited from the charity of a Winchester man who had owned farmland in Houghton. George Pemerton left a farm and lands he owned in Houghton in trust to the Corporation of the City of Winchester. The trust stipulated that various distributions were to be made annually on St George's Day out of the rents and profits from the farm. Most were made to the people of Winchester but 'fortie six shillings and eight pence' was to be paid 'yearlie for ever on St George's daie to the poore people of the parish of Houghton'.

The charity no longer exists, but throughout the 17th, 18th and 19th century money was paid by church wardens on 23 April to the poor of the village and continued to be paid until well into the 20th century.

Today the village is a picturesque beauty spot with a thriving community spirit.

Unhurried Hursley

Don't just pass through Hursley on your way to somewhere else – stop, walk around, take in the sights and drink in the history. You'll be glad you did.

TO MANY motorists, Hursley is just a brief blur of pretty buildings on the road from Winchester to Romsey. Yet anyone who decides to stop and walk around will find a well-preserved village with a fascinating history.

Hursley was home to one of the Pilgrim Fathers, who sailed to North America in 1620. Stephen Hopkins left the village to join *The Mayflower* at Southampton. His family survived the harsh climate on arrival in America better than most of their colleagues, and he became assistant governor at the pilgrims' colony during the 1630s. When Hopkins died in 1644, his English homeland was locked in a Civil War that would culminate in the execution of King Charles I.

A typical street scene in Collins Lane. (T3583L)

The former smithy.
(T3583K)

Oliver Cromwell took over the King's responsibilities, and these passed to his son, Richard, after his death in 1658. Richard was a gentleman farmer, having married into the Major family, owners of the Tudor house at Hursley Park. Catapulted from Hampshire dignitary to head of state, Richard was caught in a power struggle between the army and Parliament. The feud resulted in King Charles II taking the throne in 1660, and Richard was exiled to France. He returned to Hursley as an old man and died in 1712. He was buried in the crypt of All Saints' Church in the village, and his tomb was sealed from public view in the mid-19th century. Through a quirk of fate, the Royalist cleric who took this decision was none other than John Keble.

An Oxford University graduate and poet, Keble became famous for his no-nonsense sermons, which often made him unpopular with members of the Church hierarchy. Stan Rawdon, who has lived in Hursley since the 1970s, has produced three texts on the village's history. He says of Keble: 'Illiterate villagers who couldn't sign their own name could understand what he was getting at.'

In 1886, two decades after Keble's death, a new college at Oxford was

named in his honour. A similar tribute was paid to him in Hursley, where the primary school built in 1927 bears his name.

During the 20th century, the occupants of the Queen Anne style manor house at Hursley Park have been varied to say the least. Initially owned by the Cooper family, the manor was turned into an army camp and hospital during World War One. It was also used in World War Two, and became home to aircraft engineers working on the Spitfire fighter.

In 1958, IBM arrived, and today the company employs 3,000 people at the site. Technology developed at Hursley includes the software used by all cash machines throughout the world.

The daily influx of so many workers means that Hursley has retained several shops and two pubs, in contrast to some other Hampshire villages. The post office in Hursley is in fact so old, Mr Rawdon says, that it predates postage stamps. He adds that there is a local legend that a member of the Heathcote family, once owners of Hursley Park, slammed the penny post when it was introduced in 1840. She warned that the aristocracy was doomed now that the 'riff-raff' in the village could send messages to each other cheaply.

brides' dresses, while the vicar's stall kneeler commemorates the ministry of the Reverend Raymond Coates, who was vicar from 1969 to 1981.

The church at Little Somborne is half-Saxon and half-Norman, with the walls, windows and doorways providing evidence of both periods. Of particular interest, linking it to the present time, is the grave of Sir Thomas Sopwith, the aviation pioneer, who lived at nearby Compton Manor and died in 1989.

The 12th-century Saint Mary's Church at Ashley, now maintained by the Churches Conservation Trust, contains a triple chancel arch, a 13th-century wall painting and a 17th-century alms box cut out of an oak post.

At a time which, sadly, marks the demise of many village stores, King's

A pretty row of thatched cottages. (T3564A)

Roses in bloom at Muss Cottage. (T3564G)

filming of the TV *Worzel Gummidge* series. Cross Stores, in addition to being a well-stocked licensed store, also incorporates a post office and acts as an agent for various services and rents out videos and DVDs.

Somborne can boast two such establishments, both providing a comprehensive and friendly service. The Corner Stores has been a family-run business since its establishment in 1923 and achieved some fame in the early 1980s when used in the

Leaving the village centre along the A3057 towards Romsey brings the visitor to Horsebridge and the locality of the John of Gaunt Inn, which originally probably catered for the railway travellers following the opening of Horsebridge Station in 1865. Today it still provides sustenance for visitors, although these are now more likely to arrive by car! Sadly, the station closed in 1964 but it has undergone a metamorphosis, re-emerging as probably one of the most unusual eating venues in the south of England.

Set in two acres of land, with

King's Somborne war memorial. (T3564F)

views of river and water meadows, the attractively restored waiting room serves as a restaurant while accommodation is available in the luxury carriage of a 1922 Pullman.

Passing the John of Gaunt Inn heading towards Houghton, the more energetic visitors can join the Test Way walking route which, starting at Inkpen and finishing in Eling, follows much of the course of the River Test. The route to the left proceeds to Lower Brook, Mottisfont and on to Romsey, while the route to the right proceeds to Stockbridge and West Down.

Today, the village of King's Somborne is a mainly farming and residential area with a very strong community spirit. Over 30 active village groups cater for all ages and tastes with annual highlights including the flower show, carnival, village pantomime, harvest supper and summer and Christmas church fêtes, in addition to sporting fixtures, performances by the Somborne Singers and the services of the bell-ringers. Little wonder that the editorial team of the parish magazine, *The Gauntlet*, is never short of copy!

Thus visitors can step back in time and relive the history of this archetypal English village, while residents become part of a vibrant 21st-century community surrounded by reminders of its rich and varied past.

Standing tall. A brick and flint house. (T3564C)

Lively Littleton

WITH RACEHORSE training, sports facilities and a military base, Littleton is not everyone's idea of a sleepy Hampshire village. In fact it has always had a bit of a buzz about it, having grown up along a trade route between Andover and the South Downs.

The first inhabitants came to the area, on the north-western edge of Winchester, during the Bronze Age. A

Saunter lazily into Littleton to find the place buzzing.

burial mound in the village, known as the Disc Barrow, is believed to be 3,500 years old.

The most ancient part of St Catherine's Church is thought to be of Norman origin, which, during the early 1990s, saw a gallery built inside to increase capacity owing to the popularity of services.

The village hostelry, which prides itself on its food, is the Running Horse. Indeed, horses form a vital part of Littleton's history, with its equine training centre established in Victorian times. The Littleton Stud, which was established in 1913 and survives to this day, has produced several successful racehorses. Arguably the most famous was Lochsong, a mare renowned for her sprinting during the 1980s. But horseracing is not the only sport in Littleton. The village has 16 acres of cricket and

Ducks on Littleton Pond. (T4081B)

The Running Horse pub. (T4081P)

football pitches, along with tennis courts, a bowling green and a croquet lawn.

Austen Hooker, a retired garden centre supervisor, has lived in the village since his birth. 'I suppose we've got the best sports facilities of any village in the area,' he says. The cricket club was founded in the 1920s, their first pavilion being a converted metal box, originally designed to store warplanes. A purpose-built pavilion was put up in the 1970s.

Beside the sports pitches is the Littleton Millennium Memorial Hall, opened in 1999 after five hard years of fundraising by residents. Betty Allen, secretary of the Littleton Local History Group, says it is now the busy home of several clubs and societies. 'It's booked almost every night of the week,' she adds.

Next to the hall stands the post office, housed in a converted toilet block. Residents joke that, while small, the post office is convenient and used frequently – just like it was in its previous incarnation.

Just outside the village is the Sir John Moore Barracks, home of the Army Training Regiment. The

Flowerdown site was taken over by the Army during World War One, and later given to the Royal Air Force. During World War Two, the Royal Navy moved in, establishing HMS *Flowerdown*, a wireless station. Owing to its military links, Littleton was bombed twice in one week in the early 1940s. One attack damaged the wireless station and a nearby house, killing one woman. The second raid saw a stray bomb fall on the Littleton Stud, killing three horses.

After the war, the population of the Littleton parish expanded rapidly with the new Harestock housing estate. While many people see Harestock as part of Winchester, the residents of Littleton often take a different view. Says Austen Hooker: 'I've lived here all my life, and I see Harestock as part of Littleton.'

One popular event in the village is the Littleton Show, which takes place every September. Despite its current popularity, the show needed three bites at the cherry before

becoming a permanent fixture. In 1921, a horticultural show for Littleton, Crawley and Sparsholt was created. Moving between the villages, the event took place in July, but lasted only a few years. Two further shows were held in Littleton in 1956 and 1957, before being revived in 1971. The event has taken place every year since then. Another popular fixture – the Eve of the Eve function – was established in 1980. Every year on 23 December, residents are invited to the village hall for an evening of festive fun. Mr Hooker's wife, Connie, says it is always popular. 'If you don't get there very early, you don't get in,' she adds.

Long life Longparish

Meandering between the River Test and Harewood Forest, Longparish is ideal for gentle strolls and lazy pub lunches.

The memorial to Lanoe George Hawker, born in Longparish in 1890. (J3816L, J316L)

MOST OF Longparish was designated a conservation area in 1983 and it shows, with its surfeit of gorgeous thatched, half-timbered and white-washed cottages with gardens in vivid paintbox brights. Throw in a couple of elegant manor houses, a charming vista of meadow and church and a primary school sitting, idyllically, on the banks of the River Test, and words begin to fail.

Known as Middletun in the Domesday Book, Longparish was actually the nickname for three settlements: Forton, Middleton and East Aston. It's a classic example of linear settlements joining up to form one large village, nearly two miles long, bounded by the River Test on one side and Harewood Forest on the other – and without an obvious centre.

Church, school and village hall are clustered at one end, two pubs, village store/post office and playground at the other; and the road connecting them zigzags sharply, following ancient paths that led up from the river to the forest. As parish priest Nona Harrison puts it: 'In Longparish not everyone can walk to everything.'

That doesn't mean, however, that they haven't been united in the regeneration of the village. New groups have formed, such as the drama group. New initiatives are under way, such as a well-received plan giving every villager the opportunity to voice opinions and contribute towards its future. Church and parish council have also come together to establish a welcome group, which stages an annual get-together dinner in the village hall. The first one, in January 2004,

The mill race.
(J3816B)

The 13th-century St Nicholas's Church. (J3816H)

proved to be as much an opportunity for locals as it was for the 20-plus new arrivals to get to know each other.

Jeremy Barber, parish council chairman, believes there are plenty of other similar possibilities. Having discovered that half the residents who signed up for broadband internet services work from home in some form or other, he wonders whether they should have a weekly home-workers' social club.

The playground boasts a new addition, a skateboard ramp, and both the pubs are under relatively new management. Steve and Elaine Mancini celebrated three years of tenancy and refurbishment at the Cricketers Inn with a party, with proceeds going to the Longparish School and Community Project. They have turned this pub into a proper village local with friendly atmosphere, good home-made food and pretty gardens.

At the other end of the village, beyond the lych-gate and the remains of the old village stocks, is the church, much of it dating from the earliest years of the 13th century. Outside it looks quietly timeless with a fine perpendicular tower with embattled parapet. Inside it is unexpectedly cosy with a colourful red carpet, blue-painted ceiling over the altar and all but one of the windows of stained glass. The main east window is by Sir Edward Burne-Jones, while another, the Hawker window, is unusual in its depiction of an early airfield.

The focus on fundraising to secure the primary school's future for the next 50 years has brought everyone in the village together. 'The school is the heart of the village,' explains Jeremy Barber, 'and helps to keep the village vital.' And it is very much part of the community; for example senior citizens join the children for lunch on a monthly basis. A victim of its own success, classrooms and a new hall are now desperately needed.

On-going efforts culminated, in June 2004, in Longparish's first Gardens Festival – gardening demonstrations, craftsmen at work, games for the children and cream teas – which raised over £8,000 for the Longparish School and Community Project and drew 100 villagers together to make it happen. Fundraising continues with events like the village fête – in 2004 in the lovely setting of Longparish House – the Pumpkin Festival and the Christmas Fayre among others. Hopefully, the Garden Festival will become a regular feature, too.

The memorial window in the

A tranquil Setting. (J3816A)

church to Lanoe George Hawker, born in Longparish in 1890, celebrates the life of the first fighter pilot to win the Victoria Cross for air combat. Already bearer of the DSO for a successful attack on the Zeppelin plant at Gontrobe in April 1915, he was flying a single-seater Bristol Scout, armed only with a single-shot cavalry carbine mounted on the right side of the fuselage. He forced one German aircraft to land and brought down two more, all armed with machine guns. He died the following year after a long air battle, a victim of the German ace Baron Manfred von Richthofen, the infamous Red Baron, who said of his adversary: 'In view of the character of our fight it was clear to me that I had been tackling a flying champion.'

Delving into Micheldever

Home to a Bronze Age burial mound and scene of a tragic hanging, Micheldever is a fascinating place to visit.

FOR AN unassuming Hampshire village, Micheldever is a little quirky. The first surprise is the road to the village – a grand, sweeping stately home of an approach off the A33. It's a straight road, bordered by wide grass verges and rows of trees that create the impression of parkland. Rather than leading to some grand pile, however, it opens out into a comfortable clutter of houses that range in style from mediaeval to modern and quite a bit in between, including a pretty Victorian primary school with a clock tower straight out of Trumpton.

In fact, Micheldever also nurtures some of the most idiosyncratic mediaeval architecture in the county.

At The Crease (possibly a derivative from Cross) there's a particularly fine group of cottages clustered round a small green and one of these, a jetty hall house built in around 1475, is unique countywide for the combination of different ideas and village centre constructional techniques used in one building!

Then there's the church, St Mary the Virgin; it is quite astonishing! There's nothing like it in any other Hampshire village. This is a vast, hefty, extraordinarily impressive block of a church hidden by towering limes – more smart city than quiet village. It is dominated, not by its fine 16th-century west tower, but by an unusual, massive brick octagonal nave (built in 1806), which was designed by the architect George Dance, then working for the Baring family in neighbouring East Stratton.

Internally it is equally inspiring. The nave soars to a vaulted roof on slender Gothic pillars and in the

The village church of
St Mary the Virgin.
(F3488B)

Beautiful Bluebell Cottage is many people's dream home. (F3488D)

chancel are monuments to three of the Barings (Francis Baring, founder of the banking firm, bought Stratton House in 1740). One of these is considered to be one of the finest monuments by Flaxman.

'I attended a Christmas wedding there a few years ago when the church was lit with nothing but candle-light. It really looked impressive,' remembered George Burnand, who runs Strutt & Parker in Winchester.

Even the bustling pub, the Half Moon and Spread Eagle, next to the cricket green, is a hybrid. Originally called simply the Spread Eagle, it is said that it took on the name of a second pub in the village that burned down. It is thought to be the only pub in the country with this name and locals have resisted past attempts to change it to the more pedestrian Dever Arms.

Inside it's a comfortable mix of contemporary smart (white walls, big, simple mirrors, solid tables) and the cosily country (patterned pub carpet and wood-burning stoves) alongside a stylish menu and live music (one Friday evening each month).

'The village has it all,' added George, 'including its own river which, while not as well-known as the Itchen or the Test, has some very exciting chalk-stream fishing.'

There's a real sense of continuity in the village. Gail Giles, who came to Micheldever when she was just four, later worked in the village store, which she now owns and runs with her husband. Pam Greenwood, secretary of the popular Micheldever Variety Group, commented how there are members who joined as children who now take principal parts. With its school (boasting small classes and friendly atmosphere), thriving junior football club and playground, there's a real family feel to the village. And there's plenty for everyone to get involved with. Not only is there the Variety Club (which stages two major events a year, a play and pantomime, among other entertainments, readings and quizzes), but there are also annual fundraising events for the church including a 'Posh Picnic' and a garden open day.

Particularly tempting is the over-subscribed wine circle that meets in the village hall every month. Often they have speakers and at Christmas there's a meal, but in summer they have a special occasion when they gather in someone's back garden for champagne and strawberries. Now that conjures up a picture that's every bit as appealing as the village's slightly OTT entrance!

Micheldever has earned a place in history – and local children's text books – for the tragic hanging of a 20-year-old ploughboy, Henry Cooke, who knocked off landowner William Baring's hat during the agricultural or 'Swing' riots of 1831. He is buried at Micheldever in an unmarked grave, on which, accord-

Micheldever School. (F3488C)

ing to legend, the snow never settles. Villager Stuart Newton, however, who is involved with publishing tales chronicling Micheldever's history, suggests this may have been because the grave was sited near the Bake-house wall.

This area has been inhabited for thousands of years and remains of a Roman villa in Micheldever Wood, a Saxon cemetery at Weston Farm and traces of still earlier occupants in an oval-shaped barrow used as a Bronze Age burial site have been discovered.

Keeping the village supplied. (F3488F)

Bolting Baddesley

DURING THE 20th century, the population in what was a small rural village exploded into the large modern place it is today, but the historical legacy of North Baddesley, near Romsey, is intriguing and vast.

When an order of knights came to town, they put the village on the map. The Knights of St John of Jerusalem, later known as the Knights Hospitaller, moved into the village in 1167, a mediaeval order dedicated to the care and protection of pilgrims, tending the sick and infirm, including crusaders in their quest to return the Holy Land to the Christian world.

A Europe-wide order, they became extremely wealthy land-owners thanks to the patronage of rich and noble families. They acquired the overlordship rights to the manor in around 1304 and rededicated the little All Saints' Church to St John the Baptist, their patron saint.

The Black Death of 1348–49 resulted in the transfer of the Hospitallers' Hampshire HQ from Godsfield, near Alresford, to North Baddesley. They were there until the early 16th century, when Henry VIII dissolved the monasteries and their possessions were forfeit to the Crown.

Poachers, yes, but knights, treason and stampeding horses are things people would not normally associate with a village like North Baddesley, near Romsey, but it all happened there.

A famous owner of the Manor after the knights was Sir Thomas Seymour, who acquired it in 1539. His sister, Jane, was Henry's third wife and mother of Edward VI.

A delightful stroll.
(T3481H)

The church of St John the Baptist, with the two gravestones commemorating Charles Smith on the right. (T3841L)

A tad more peaceful than their 20th-century cousins. (T3481C)

Shady days. (T3841D)

When Henry died in 1547, Thomas's brother, Edward, Duke of Somerset, became the protector of the young Edward, and Thomas was made Lord High Admiral and Baron Seymour of Sudley. Thereafter he tried to supplant his brother as guardian of the then King Edward. In 1547 he married Henry's widow, Catherine Parr, and was influential in securing an Act of Parliament in the same year that made the duration of the protectorate dependent on 'the King's pleasure' instead of being fixed until the King was 18, and he carefully cultivated Edward's friendship. After his wife's death in 1548, he was unsuccessful in gaining Princess Elizabeth's hand in marriage and his activities provoked questioning by the Privy Council. He was convicted of high treason and executed. During Elizabethan times an E-shaped manor house was built, but was later severely damaged by fire and was replaced by a Georgian-style building in 1789. It is now in private ownership.

Jumping forward a couple of hundred years to 1822, a poaching incident resulted in a man being hanged and commemorated by two tombstones in St John's churchyard. Robert Snelgrove, an assistant keeper on the Broadlands Estate, then belonging to Lord Palmerston, found two men poaching in Hough Coppice, near Toothill. Toothill was then in North Baddesley but is now in the neighbouring parish of Rownhams. Snelgrove was only a boy and unarmed, and Charles Smith, aged 29, discharged his gun at Snelgrove, who was wounded but did not die. Smith was not caught until a year after the incident, and he stood trial at Winchester and was condemned to death by Mr Justice Burroughs and was hanged. The first gravestone was erected by William Cobbett, writer and social reformer of the time, who felt that Smith had been a victim of oppression. The second appeared many years after Lord Palmerston's death and was erected by his grandson, Colonel Evelyn Ashley, in an attempt to absolve the family from any blame. Looking at the village now and seeing how suburban it has become, it is difficult to think all these stories originated in its infancy.

Weather vane on the village hall. (T3841F)

Proud owners

North Waltham has altered little in the last century – and is partly owned by its population.

THE PEOPLE of North Waltham, near Basingstoke, are very proud of their village. They are also part of it. For, apart from their own properties, they own a large chunk of it. Villagers are in the unique position of owning Cuckoo Meadow, a piece of open land donated 50 years ago by landowner William Rathbone, which is used for recreation. And nothing is done to that land until everyone has had their say, and the way it is today reflects the wishes of the whole community down the years.

2004 was North Waltham's golden jubilee heritage year, marking the village trust, which oversees the

Street scene. (J3624J)

The village pond. (J324F)

ownership of the meadow. A heritage trail has been established, accompanied by a leaflet as well as a book using pictures from the extensive village archive, making its history accessible to all. This was all made possible through funding from the National Lottery and the Local Heritage Initiative.

Led by Richard Tanner, village archivist and chairman of the North Waltham, Steventon, Ashe and Dean History Society, children from North Waltham Primary School designed the trail. Mr Tanner, whose book is called *North Waltham Then and Now*, was working on a talking book. He said: 'It is a way of taking some of the archive, which is vast, and showing it and making it accessible to people.' This portable archive reveals other fascinating facts about North Waltham.

Its early Anglo-Saxon name suggests a Romano-British origin and the centrepiece of the village, literally, is the pond. Home to ducks, who have their own road crossing signs, the pond is 10 metres above the water table and is fed by an intermittent spring. This attractive natural feature is complemented by buildings dating back to mediaeval times which surround it.

Rose Cottage is North Waltham's oldest house, dating from 1460,

opposite which is the heavily timbered, 16th-century Walnut Lodge. The main watering hole is the Fox pub at the top of the village, which is host to many a social event. Other pubs are the Wheatsheaf – where Jane Austen, who lived in neighbouring Steventon, would collect the family mail and which, more latterly, was home to the girl who became Lady Lucan – at the entrance to the village and the

Rising Sun, towards the back of the village.

Everyone is willing to help if they are needed, either for fundraising to buy new equipment for the children's play park on Cuckoo Meadow or on parish council issues. North Waltham is the kind of village that wouldn't need street lights, even if it had them. The village is home to 670 people, an increase of only 300 people since 1901.

It is a sleepy place for the most part during the day, but this adds to its tranquillity, nestled into the north Hampshire countryside. The shop is the only amenity in the village, the post office having closed some time ago, but it serves the community well and is within walking distance for most people.

Adele Stevenson is a young mum who lives in the village with her husband and children. She is a member of the parish council, has helped develop the village plan and has been involved in the process of setting up a website for the council. She said: 'I like being able to walk my dog at 10 o'clock at night and feel safe.'

Sleepy tranquillity is the order of the day in North Waltham. (J3624G)

Disparate twins

Nursling and Rownhams have been together now for many years but they could be chalk and cheese.

DOWNSTREAM from Romsey on the River Test lies the parish of Nursling and Rownhams, two villages joined at the hip but definitely chalk and cheese. Until the 1970s, Rownhams was a small collection of cottages, clustered around the Victorian St John's Church. Since then, several estates have been built, creating an atmosphere of suburbia.

In contrast, historians believe the first settlement was established in Nursling nearly 2,000 years ago. The Romans bridged the Test here and founded a village called Onna,

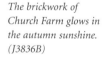
The brickwork of Church Farm glows in the autumn sunshine. (J3836B)

although nothing has survived to the present day. Also gone without trace is the monastery, which was destroyed by Danish raiders in 878. Many years earlier, it was home to the parish's most famous resident.

Born at Crediton, in Devon, in around 680, Winfrith, later to become St Boniface, came to Nursling as a 14-year-old. A gifted scholar and preacher, he spent over 20 years at the monastery, where he was ordained as a priest in 710. In 722, he arrived in Rome to volunteer his services to Pope Gregory II, who gave him the name Boniface, meaning 'doer of good'.

Boniface then spent three decades converting German tribes to Christianity. He was canonised as a saint after heathen warriors murdered him in Friesland in 755. In recognition of his work, Boniface was chosen as the patron saint of Germany... not bad for a Hampshire priest.

Closer to home, the 13th-century St Boniface's Church, built on the probable site of the monastery, is named in his honour. He is also the patron saint of brewers, and there are plenty of places in Nursling and Rownhams to raise a glass to his memory.

The Four Horseshoes in Nursling Street has a vast beer garden and

Taking it easy. (J3836E)

offers several real ales. The Balmoral Inn at Romsey Road is a Beefeater pub, popular with families, party-goers, and guests at the adjoining motel. Just 50 yards away stands the Horns Inn. The bar is a pleasing bustle of parish gossip, while the restaurant provides a friendly place to dine. Golfing enthusiasts are also catered for as, while the name is a tad misleading, Romsey Golf Club is actually in Nursling and Rownhams.

Other leisure attractions include the Toothill Observatory, operated

A view of the River Test. (J3836J)

by the Solent Amateur Astronomers Society, which is open at least one weekend every month and to be found above the subterranean reservoir in Upper Toothill Road. The observatory was built in 1981, which makes it around 400 years younger than Grove Place. This grand property in Upton Lane is one of the finest examples of Elizabethan architecture in Hampshire, and is currently used as a private school.

Julia Gundry chairs the Nursling and Rownhams History Group and has lived in the parish for over 30 years. During that time, she has witnessed one of the largest population increases anywhere in Hampshire. For her, the impact has come from the motorway.

It was during the mid-1970s that six lanes of tarmac were driven through the north-eastern side of the parish. After the M27 and M271 were opened, Nursling and Rownhams expanded quickly, owing to the new road links and proximity to Southampton. Nonetheless, the parish offers a popular combination of friendly village life coupled with modern city services nearby.

There is an added bonus in that several shops in Nursling and Rownhams have seen added support through the population increase. 'We are very handy for everything down here but still very rural,' Julia explains.

The arrival of the motorway age has certainly put the parish on the map. It definitely makes life easier for any German tourists who want to find the ancestral home of their patron saint.

Bourne to great names

NOW BETTER known to many as a conurbation running alongside the M3, Otterbourne in the past has seen such luminaries as Sir Isaac Newton, John Keble and Victorian writer Charlotte Yonge.

Little needs to be said about Newton – except that the village is unlikely to be the place where he famously sat under an apple tree. And Keble needs little introduction as the man who gave his name to an Oxford college – though many may not be aware that he was once vicar of the parish church, St Matthew's,

When it comes to celebrities, Hampshire has had its share down the ages, and Otterbourne is no exception.

built in 1838, when Charlotte was 15, and was a leader of the Oxford Movement, which called for a return to High Church Anglicanism. Among hymns he penned are *New Every Morning.*

Charlotte Yonge, in her day, was a major celebrity, a prolific writer who

The Old Forge Inn. (T4237)

outside of Elderfield House, to which the Yonge family later moved. Otterbourne lies on the route of an old Roman road between Venta Belgarum and Clausentum, or Winchester and Southampton as they are now known.

The Otterbourne that Sir Isaac Newton would have known while lodging at Cranbury House in his twilight years was a sleepy, rural hamlet. A century later, the village would suffer a rude awakening due to a revolution in Britain's transport network. In 1840, the London to Southampton railway line opened for business. While it brought prosperity to some places, it was the death knell for old Otterbourne.

Michael Warne, chairman of the parish council, said: 'It was the M3 extension through Twyford Down of its day – an environmental disaster.'

produced over 100 books, including *The Heir of Redclyffe*, which is still in print. She was born in Otterbourne House, a three-storey 18th-century villa that is still a landmark on the main road. It's also possible to see the

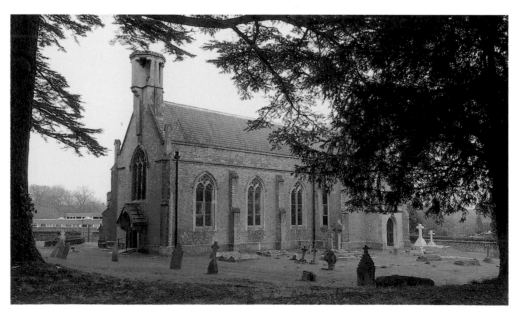

The line created so much noise that the villagers who had not already moved swiftly packed their bags.

Within half a century, the village had moved half a mile east to its present location. Hardly anything of old Otterbourne survives. Even the mediaeval church in Kiln Lane fell victim to the railway, closing soon after it arrived. But one thing changes little – the reason it became Otterbourne. A stream, the Otter Bourne, still rises nearby and still flows through the village before joining the Itchen at Brambridge.

Elderfield House, Otterbourne, the home of Victorian novelist Charlotte Yonge. (T4237G)

The cared sign at the bottom of Otterbourne Hill. (T4237F)

Race fit Ropley

Most people view Ropley as a ribbon conurbation alongside the A31, but not only does it have a heart, it has plenty of 'go', too.

THERE'S A decidedly competitive streak to the picturesque village of Ropley. Its hub is tucked away around three-quarters of a mile away from the busy main drag of the A31 – which runs between Winchester and Alton – a community which revels in its games and competitions.

Most renowned, perhaps, is the annual pram race, the proceeds of which all go into the village coffers and which in 2005 celebrates its 40th year. It has teams of two (who push and sit alternately), who whistle round a circuit of the village every bank holiday Monday in spring in as quick a time as possible. Perhaps unsurprisingly, none of them baulks at the regulation stop at the Chequers

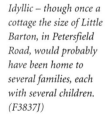

Idyllic – though once a cottage the size of Little Barton, in Petersfield Road, would probably have been home to several families, each with several children. (F3837J)

pub, one of two inns in Ropley, and one of two compulsory drink stops.

'It brings everyone together and it's a social thing,' explained Tim Day, the village archivist, who has lived in Ropley since 1965. He believes the race, which started as a bet, is unique in the UK and has a good chance of entering the Guinness Book of Records.

However, he said the types of vehicles entering today were not quite the same as in the old days. 'You get a lot of Formula One prams and hybrids with bicycle wheels,' he pointed out.

As well as rumours of welly-throwing competitions in the late 1970s, village folklore has it, as recorded by resident Marianna Hagen in the annals of Old Ropley in 1929, that two farmers had a race two centuries ago to find out who had the fastest horses. Carrying half-ton lumps of stone, the men raced each other from the other side of nearby Four Marks in wagons to see who could carry the stone furthest.

The winner managed to carry the heavy load to Hall Place on the Petersfield Road, while the runner-up only managed as far as Gascoigne Lane – where the stone is still buried in the hedge today. The prize-winning stone, and a plaque to com-memorate its origins, are displayed

Cross purposes – the 15.23 departure to Alton on the left and the 15.23 train for Alresford on the right. Thanks to keen conservationists, Ropley still has an operational station, and is an important part of the Watercress Line as it is home to the loco shed, which can be seen in the background. (F3837A)

Ropley House on Berry Hill is a restored early Georgian house constructed in red brick with blue brick bands. (F3837K)

on the recreation ground next to the village hall.

Marianna Hagen appears to have taken a keen interest in the male antics in the village, and was a noteworthy figure. This upstanding Victorian lady lived at Meadowside, a large house at the centre of the village, near the thriving primary school and just down the road from the beautiful, originally Norman church of St Peter.

Early 20th-century post box with 21st-century information – the George V letter box in Hammonds Lane (F3837F)

Marianna was fed up with all the men drinking in the local hostelries and took matters into her own hands by building a temperance room on to her house, where no alcohol could be consumed. Today the busy Coffee Room is hired out for parties, Horticultural Society meetings, children's clubs, church meetings and line dancing!

A few paces up on Lyeway Lane is the former home of another equally pious figure. Archbishop's Cottage was where William Howley, who went on to become the Archbishop of Canterbury, was born. His father, also William, was the vicar of Ropley. Archbishop Howley crowned William IV king in 1830 and Victoria queen in 1837.

Also on a royal note, another of Ropley's claims to fame is that hives from the area, popular for bee-keeping in years gone by, were used to supply William the Conquerer with honey for mead making.

But, arguably, the village is best-known to thousands of people as one of the stops on the Mid-Hants Railway, the Watercress Line, the preserved steam railway, decommissioned as a branch line in the seventies and now run by volunteers. While the line's headquarters are at Alresford, Ropley is the engineering centre.

Other track lovers who use the village as a base for their pastime are the many ramblers who come to Ropley to experience some of the 40 or so footpaths that criss-cross the village, often using the village hall as a starting point.

Each Boxing Day morning, villagers and their families and friends take advantage of the network for a festive stroll in an annual walk for village funds. This year will be the 31st Christmas outing but there are plenty of paths to try out for a good few years to come – and hopefully much more money to be raised!

Ropley is as much a thriving village today as it has been for many centuries, and despite rocketing house prices meaning it's increasingly difficult for young people to stay in the village, there are moves afoot to build more affordable homes. 'People who leave Ropley always want to come back,' said Tim.

It would be worth living there for the pram race alone!

Shedding light. (F3837G)

Special Soberton

ON THE secluded eastern flank of the meandering Meon, where chalk downland meets ancient woodland, Soberton lies hidden from view by high banks down narrow lanes. This village offers an opportunity to lose yourself among a convergence of footpaths, bridleways and a cycleway; for this is where the Wayfarers' Walk, Soberton and Newtown Millennium Walk and the Meon Valley Trail (a cycle route along a disused railway) merge.

Escape to the peace of Soberton in the Meon Valley – but bring your walking boots or bike.

Here is a thoroughly delightful way to waste a Sunday. The comparatively little-known Meon Valley is lush, heavily wooded and full of hidden treats – particularly the profusion of little ancient churches scattered on watermeadow and

The long-distance Wayfarers' Walk passes through Soberton. (T3665K)

St Peter's Church, Soberton. (T36651)

valleyside. A brief visit feels like a holiday... as if you've escaped.

Soberton itself is the quintessential English village settled around a village green. On one side there's the picturesque church, dating mostly from the 12th and 13th century and adorned by a chequerboard patterned tower in flint and stone. Adjacent to it is a proper country pub, the White Lion, with a classic Georgian front hiding a rambling mediaeval structure. On the other side of the green, dominating the approach from Droxford, is the large late 19th-century Soberton Towers, with stone-dressed battlemented facades.

Overall, the village has changed little in appearance over the decades, but the people have. This was once a naval village – a precedent established by Baron Soberton, who retired here having, in his last command as

Commodore Anson, destroyed the French fleet off Finistère in 1747. But now Soberton is full of young families – presumably not attracted by the facilities, as there is neither village shop nor primary school.

'Soberton, while having that out of the way feel, also benefits from so much being so close by – such as the coast and towns,' comments George Burnand, who runs Strutt & Parker in Winchester.

Lulled into the languid peace of a Sunday morning, the quiet only disturbed by the steady preparations of Graham, the pub landlord, and his two collies (an endearingly boisterous pup, Bonzo, and Mr Spike, resigned to the antics of the irritating youngster), you could be forgiven for assuming nothing ever happens here. Even the landlord comments jovially that there are more horses than people in Soberton (he owns two horses himself – and they're a great hit with the kids). You would be wrong, however. If you wanted you could be out every night of the week, there are so many groups and societies, like the History Society, Conservation Society, the Soberton Players and the Meon Valley Self-sufficiency Group, who meet in the village.

Of particular interest is the 3P's Society, once the St Peter's Parish Planners, started by the Revd Roger Moseley, and now a jolly good excuse for a get-together, with activities as diverse as concerts, dinners, a pre-Wimbledon tennis tournament and a day at the races.

It is a society that reflects the dynamic role of the church within this community. The relatively new incumbent, the Revd Stuart Holt, who came to the parish just under a year ago, continues this proactive approach – particularly in providing for the parish's youngsters. And this is a big parish, covering the old village of Soberton, predominantly Victorian Soberton Heath and self-explanatory Newtown as well as much of the Forest of Bere. It is claimed that this is the largest parish in the country and, getting lost among the endless country roads, it certainly feels like it.

Alongside more traditional fare, such as summer fêtes, the church ensures there is plenty for the younger part of the community. The first week of the summer holidays is the annual children's week and, this April, a new youth club started in Soberton Heath.

Now Mr Holt is busy planning a 'battle of the bands' programme involving local record producers and professional musicians. 'There is a great need for this sort of thing in the rural community,' he explains, adding, 'this is an area that's actually considered disadvantaged because of geographical access.'

For those of us in search of solitude, geographical inaccessibility is a bonus rather than a hindrance. It certainly doesn't stop the White Lion

Graham Acres, landlord of the White Lion at Soberton, with his collies, Bonzo and Mr Spike. (T3665A)

filling up steadily with regulars and visitors alike – all greeted indiscriminately by Bonzo, eager to chew as many shoelaces as possible.

They come in search of an old-fashioned local: friendly landlord, easy conversation, a quiet read of the papers, and good beer (a couple are local, including one brewed especially for the pub by the Hampshire Brewery). And they find it – although, with a nod to technology, you can also work on your laptop in the bar.

One regular, who comes from some miles distant, says the pub's charm lies in it being the 'sort of pub you can come into very occasionally and you'll always be included and welcomed'.

And, similarly, it's probably the sort of village that you can visit very occasionally and always feel at home.

Secret Sparsholt

A MOST extraordinary aspect of Sparsholt is that there is still a village accessible only by narrow, single-track lanes to be found so close to a city centre. Wander off the main thoroughfares west of Winchester and you are suddenly in deep countryside, surrounded by hedgerows, meadows and woodland. This sense of being transported so immediately into the rural landscape never ceases to amaze.

This village's name comes from the Anglo-Saxon for 'spar', meaning straight timber, and 'holt' meaning managed woodland.

From Pitt, Sparsholt is discovered beyond the Crab Woods (particularly enchanting in May, carpeted with deep swathes of bluebells). It is a tightly grouped village gathered

The Plough Inn at Sparsholt. (T3506M)

around its church, St Stephen's, which stands on an elevated site opposite the village shop, Memorial Hall and primary school – all jostling for space beside or behind each other. Once the Woodman pub was adjacent to this little cluster, but this has long been a residence. Now the only pub is on the outskirts, the Plough, and it is well known for delicious, good-value food in a traditional country pub setting.

St Stephen's, a typical Hampshire church of flint and stone, is a tardis, much bigger, wider and lighter inside than expected and quite delightful in its simplicity. The school is a clever mix of old and new with a contemporary extension faced in traditional flint and brick.

Particularly striking, however, is the village store and post office: 'marvellous, very friendly and stocking a little bit of everything' said one villager, 'a lifesaver' added another.

Housed in the old Well House (built in 1897 to mark the diamond jubilee of Queen Victoria), it is unbelievably quaint. The overhead tank has become a storage room and the pump room is now a dolls' house of a shop. It's run by three friends who, more or less, have been running the shop between them for 10 years this December and are responsible for the welcoming atmosphere.

Overall, the village has remained largely untouched with only a little infilling over recent years. The

Picturesque cottage with a homely feel. (T3506L)

greater change is, inevitably, in the nature of the community. This was once a farming community boasting seven or eight dairies. Now the only dairy herd is at the local agricultural college, which moved to its current premises on the edge of the village in 1914. Back then there were only around 30 or so students; now there are more than 1,300 full-time and 6,000 part-time students.

Sparsholt has become popular with commuters, who revel in finding a village that is tucked away like a secret yet so close to a mainline station and motorway. Such close proximity to Winchester, however, ensures that facilities such as the school, cricket team and WI all thrive, attracting members and pupils from outside the locality.

'Being a short drive from the station, Sparsholt is one of the most frequently named villages when potential purchasers request areas they are looking to buy within,' says George Burnand, of Strutt and Parker. He adds: 'Sparsholt had a large part to play in my agricultural interests, I remember the college having a herd of Jersey cows, watching piglets being born and feeding the lambs. It really brings back memories.'

This is a small village with a lot of soul. Volunteers provide a meal every week for Winchester's Night Shelter and there's a registered charity, the Gwen Bush Foundation, established by villager Edmund Bush, to raise funds for research into pain relief (less than 1 percent of all medical research funding goes into pain research). You'll also discover one-off concerts at the church alongside the more usual fare of summer fêtes and harvest suppers. There has even been an open day to recruit bellringers to join the happy band.

Otherwise villagers can take their pick from badminton to bridge, and from the history society (running for nine years) to the new Hog the Limelight scheme (encompassing children's workshops and salsa dancing for adults) to encourage activities for villagers.

But however busy this village may be, quietly, behind the banks and hedges, the abiding impression is of peace and solitude against a backdrop of buttercups and birdsong.

Manors maketh St Mary

It's amazing what beauty can be found in Hampshire if you keep off the main roads, as you can discover on a run through the Andover area.

ST MARY BOURNE once comprised five manors: Binley, Egbury, Week, Stoke and St Mary Bourne, all of which were included in the Manor of Hurstbourne Priors.

In 1565 Sir Robert Oxenbridge, owner of Hurstbourne Priors, was ordered to prove by what title he held the five manors; a law suit was begun to determine whether or not they were manors in their own right. It

A sign outside a blacksmith's shop. (J4132G)

The George Inn in the village centre. (J4132E)

*A thatched terrace in
the village centre.
(J4132J)*

*The heart of St Mary
Bourne village.
(J4132K)*

was finally judged that from time immemorial they had been hamlets of Hurstbourne Priors, and Sir Robert therefore obtained a recognition of his title to them.

A local tradition maintains that Queen Elizabeth I stayed at Valley Farm, Stoke. The Church of St Peter dates from about 1157 and contains one of the rarest ecclesiastical treasures in Hampshire, a black marble font at least 800 years old, brought from Tournai in Belgium. This font is one of only four in Hampshire and is regarded as one of the finest in the country. Recessed into the south wall of the church is the 14th-century effigy of a crusader knight, thought to be one of the Oxenbridges.

St Mary Bourne used to be considered such a healthy place to live that it was said 'those born in the village would live as long as they liked'. Certainly the burial register for the last century shows a large proportion of people living to well over 90, and in one case to 100 years old. The 'Bourne Revel' was a celebrated festival in the 18th century, at which young men tried their skill at wrestling, single-stick and back sword, which resulted in bruised shins and crowns.

A long since dried-up tributary of the Bourne stream. (J4132H)

Sweet Charity

EVERY SO often you stumble, unexpectedly, across somewhere wonderful. Stoke Charity is a forgotten treasure, left undisturbed in an area of the county, north of Winchester, that is often referred to as Hidden Hampshire. Main roads (M3 and A33 to the east, A34 to the west and A303 to the north) career around its perimeter and the main Southampton to London rail line bisects it. But, in spite of this, there is an air of tranquillity.

Put on your walking shoes and explore the village of Stoke Charity.

'I recently attended a barbecue in the village,' recalls George Burnand, who has lived in the area all his life and now runs Strutt & Parker in Winchester. 'I realised that it is one of not many villages that has great transport communications, but is not affected by any of them.'

A family afternoon out for the swan and her cygnets in front of St Mary's Church. (J3443B)

I came across the village – a mere cluster of cottages on a fold of the chalk downlands, on an early summer evening. Retracing my steps, having taken the wrong way, I discovered a view so serene it wowed me – if you can be wowed quietly.

It was the sort of scene that appears in photographs, but is rarely found to be so perfect in reality. In the setting sun, the creamy oak-shingled tower and splayed spire of St Mary and St Michael rose above water meadows with rowing boats casually abandoned on the banks of

A splash of summer colour. (J3443E)

the River Dever. It may be small, but Stoke Charity is a treasure trove of architectural surprises and its church is foremost among them. It is the most perfect little church cast adrift among fields.

Simon Jenkins, in his book, *England's Thousand Best Churches*,

Staddlestones adorn this cottage garden. (J3443G)

*The banks of the river
Dever. (J3443A)*

awarded it a coveted two stars. He writes: 'The interior is astonishing, brightly scrubbed Norman, not over-restored and with a wealth of mediaeval monuments... which so litter the place that the visitor is in danger of falling over them.

'The walls and floors are rich in mediaeval fragments, tiles, carvings, mouldings and archaeological bric-a-brac. A light, happy museum of a church.'

The building mainly dates from the 12th and 13th century and benefited from major restoration work in the 1990s – financed primarily by the local community. Fundraising activities and village occasions are ongoing, featuring each year, around the middle of May, a weekend of events that starts on Friday with a lunch in aid of Barnardo's in a marquee at The Old Rectory.

This is followed on the Saturday with a village celebration, including barbecue, raffles and competitions. This year's event was particularly special as it included a ceremony to remember Mary Adams, post-mistress in the village for 37 years, who died recently; helium balloons were released by village children at the bench, on the village green, which had been purchased by the village in her name.

Finally, on the Sunday, there was a concert in the church by Madding Crowd, which attracted over 100 people and raised around £750 for the church.

George Burnand first came across 'this cracking village' when attending a NADFAS event at quite a young age. 'It included a number of activities, one of which was a nature walk round the village and a visit to the church. It left a lasting impression on me,' he said.

This is a village that not only remembers its long-time residents, but takes care of its newcomers, too. Ruth Guy only moved to Stoke Charity two years ago (to a house which was once at the centre of watercress production in the village), but within three days of arriving, John and Sally Martin organised a drinks party for them and absolutely everyone in the village came.

'Stoke Charity is remarkable for its village feel,' commented Ruth. 'Another annual village event is the carol service followed by a drinks party – it's a good excuse to get everyone together.

'The village feels as though it's in a time warp,' she added. 'You know that towns and villages are often twinned? Well, the joke round here is that Stoke Charity is twinned with heaven.'

Great Scotney!

Don't drive on by Sutton Scotney, make a detour. This is a village with lots going on…

How many villages have an old fire station like this? (T3508L)

IT MAY not be entirely chocolate-box gorgeous, but Sutton Scotney does possess areas of intense prettiness with timber-framed thatched cottages, ochre-washed walls, weatherboard detailing and gardens overspilling with lavender. Even the old fire station, in use until 1972 and now a store for the Coach and Horses, is thatched and quaint.

What it lacks in looks, Sutton Scotney makes up for in amenities. There's a farm shop, surgery (including dispensary), post office and petrol station (anybody who has lived in splendid rural isolation will know what a find these facilities are). There's also the Gratton, a massive leisure area, including playground, tennis courts and cricket pitch (plus a new pavilion in the offing). And there is still a fire service, part-time, but active! 'Sutton Scotney is underplayed' suggests one villager, 'perhaps because it is not purely decorative… it's a real hubbub of a place.'

It's convenient, too. Stretched along a convergence of roads and boarded by the River Dever on one side and the A34 on the other, Sutton Scotney boasts easy access to major road networks in all directions. Yet you can quickly walk down the road and disappear along the footpaths and bridleways that stretch away into the fields for miles.

In particular, however, Sutton Scotney has a dynamic community spirit – a legacy, perhaps, of current and previous owners of Sutton Manor Estate. Lord and Lady Rank,

Egypt Cottage on the northern edge of Sutton Scotney. (T3508H)

for example, were great benefactors, giving the village, in 1965, the aforementioned Gratton Surgery. Sutton Manor is now a nursing home whose owner has allowed Wessex Children's Hospice Trust to lease land (for a rent of a dozen red roses on Midsummer's Day) and build Naomi House for terminally ill children.

These businesses are the heart of the village in more ways than one as they also provide employment opportunities for locals, helping the village reinvent itself from estate village, with a sideline in coaching inns, to a contemporary community.

In comparison Greenways farm shop is in its infancy, at just a year and a half old, but expanding monthly. Run by Colin Hutchings, it is housed in what appears to be an unobtrusive hut with attached nursery. Inside it's lovely – all wooden floorboards, dressers and wicker baskets. There's a broad mix of essentials and treats. Colin always tries to source produce from the area or grow his own, but he also ensures he offers what the community needs – so you'll find bananas alongside Hampshire asparagus. Look out for local organic chicken and home-baked cakes and quiches – in short whatever you need for a simple supper or a flamboyant dinner party. 'I can vouch for that,' says George Burnand of Strutt & Parker, who heard about the shop at a dinner party. 'After catching a brown trout in the Dever, we were treated to not only the fish, but also an array of fresh vegetables from Greenways.'

A quiet corner of the village. (T3508E)

At the centre of the community, with little doubt, is Victoria Hall (opened in 1897 to mark Queen Victoria's diamond jubilee), which reopened in 2001 following renovation and expansion. Villagers consider Sue Lane, clerk to the parish council, to be a driving force behind the village hall. There are some 14 or so regular groups held in the hall from art and bridge classes to the WI, yoga and youth clubs and everything in between – including parents and toddlers.

For many it provides the local entertainment. 'The village hall has really taken off,' explains Sue, 'We had The Hollies the other week and it was a sell-out. Sutton Scotney has a buzz about it'. Sue continues, 'it's a nice, mixed community and we really do try to look after each other.'

Locals recall the Bypass Party held on the A34 prior to its opening in 1981 – making a huge difference to the quality of life in Sutton Scotney at that time. Current village get-togethers include the summer fête (10 July at Wonston), a massive event that encompasses the parish, not just the village. Also the Gratton Trust stages fundraising activities year-round, including a jazz festival in June, a village fun day (31 July) – which has succeeded the spectacular carnivals that some villagers remember back in the sixties – and an auction of promises (2 October).

With thanks to Peter Clarke's recently published *Dever & Down*, a history of the Parish of Wonston.

Colourful cottage garden in the centre of the village. (T3508K)

Wandering Wellow

THE COMBINED parish of East and West Wellow lies three miles west of Romsey and adds up to a large spread of woods and commons on the River Blackwater and its tributaries. The

Wander the byways of Wellow, once home to one of Britain's greatest daughters.

The Foxes Lane ford across the River Blackwater. (T4111G)

A wonderful autumn treescape on West Wellow Common. (T4111F)

large, scattered village of West Wellow is on the A36, while the smaller East Wellow boasts a 13th-century church, which contains some wall paintings from that date.

In the churchyard is the memorial tombstone of Florence Nightingale, who lived for many years at Embley Park, a large Elizabethan-style mansion which is now a school. The grounds retain much of the original plant collections of rhododendrons and other exotic species. The Nightingale family bought the Embley Park estate at Wellow in around 1825 because Mrs Nightingale wanted somewhere warm to go to – their main home was in Derbyshire – and to be closer to London.

So the woman who would later be famous for raising nursing to the level of a respectable profession spent much of her childhood at Embley Park, and the village of Wellow benefited greatly from the family's generosity.

They paid for the school to be built, which is thriving today, and

Florence was heavily involved in helping the poor community of the village. She adored her studies and was tutored by her father, William, to become proficient in mathematics, languages and the arts. Religion, too, played a big part in her life, and it was while sitting out in the gardens of Embley Park that she had what she described as her 'calling' – she heard the voice of God calling her to do his work. At the time she had no idea of what this was to be but the rest, of course, is history.

In 1850, Florence began her nurse's training at the Institute of St

A pregnant Jenny on Canada Common. (T4111C)

Vincent de Paul in Alexandria, Egypt, a hospital run by the Roman Catholic Church. At the outbreak of the Crimean War in 1854, she was asked by her friend Sidney Herbert, the British Secretary of War, to oversee the introduction of nurses to military hospitals. On her return to England, she continued her hospital reforms and helped with the design of hospitals – one of them being the Royal Hampshire County Hospital at Winchester.

Florence died in 1910 at the age of 90. In her will she asked to be buried in a simple ceremony at the family vault at St Margaret's Church, at Wellow. Her tombstone bears only the initials F.N.

Away from the world of nursing, and its most famous daughter, the village of Wellow is also renowned for its ice-cream parlour, Carlo's. Italian family the Donnarummas ran an ice-cream making business in Southampton. When World War Two broke out they, like many from the city, went into the country during the evenings to escape the ferocious bombing. They came to Wellow and liked it so much that they stayed. The head of the family, Carlo, established his business here and the home-made ice cream became incredibly popular. Over the years, his son, also named Carlo, took over the business and today it is as strong as ever. Carlo's Ices and Tea Rooms does exactly 'what it says on the tin' and there is also an area where animals are kept, to the delight of the younger visitors.

As with many rural communities, Wellow has shifted from being a working village to somewhere where people want to live while working elsewhere. There is, however, an active social scene and the village hall is always busy with some activity or another. Villagers also have the privilege of owning their own common, Canada Common, which backs on to the New Forest. This is well used by local dog walkers and those from further afield, as well as ponies!

Carlo Donnarumma outside his ice cream parlour. (T4111A)

Lord above

On the face of it, West Meon is a typical sleepy Hampshire village but do a bit of digging and it's history is interesting – if diverse.

'ONE FAMOUS and one infamous,' is the way local historian, Ray Stone, describes two of the occupants of the graveyard at St John the Evangelist's church at West Meon.

Buried in front of the impressive flint church, which rests high above the rest of the village, is Thomas Lord – the man who founded the famous London cricket ground which still bears his name. Tucked away almost in the undergrowth behind the church is one Guy Francis De Moncy Burgess – one of the Cambridge ring, spies who became secret agents for Russia. Burgess grew up in the village, where his father was a naval officer.

Ray (72), who's lived in West

The village war memorial. (T3597D)

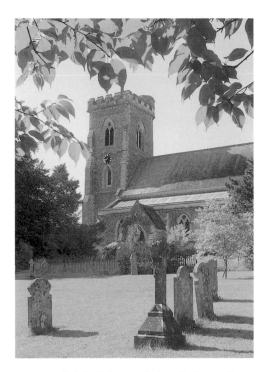

St John the Baptist church. (T3597A)

Meon all his life, explained that when the disgraced spy's ashes were brought back to the village after his death in 1963, the family wanted it to be kept quiet. 'They were worried that someone would come and wreck the gravestone, but it's been alright for 40 years – it's water under the bridge now.' By contrast, Thomas Lord's final resting place has always been a point of celebration for this cricket-loving village.

Lord, a Yorkshireman, retired to the village and died there in 1832, aged 76, after selling the ground he'd established in St John's Wood to the Marylebone Cricket Club. In 1951, the MCC had a newly inscribed stone slab placed over his grave and, in August 1955, the London club took on the village team – which still plays every Sunday – in a celebratory match to commemorate the 200th anniversary of Lord's birth. The match went the Londoners' way. 'One member of the 1955 team remarked it was like playing head office,' said Ray.

As a testament to arguably the village's most famous son, one of the pubs in the High Street, previously the New Inn, was renamed the Thomas Lord. The pub today is brimming with all manner of willow and leather artefacts in tribute to this most English of games.

But cricket wasn't always so popular in the village. Archdeacon Bayley, who became rector in 1826, tried to ban villagers from playing the game on Sunday afternoons and introduced a service after lunch. But his attempt failed as the labourers would go to church, taking their kit with them, and dash to the field as soon as the last hymn was sung.

An ambitious man, the Archdeacon's plans for West Meon are still plain to see. The large, Gothic church, which once saw up to 600 worshippers at a service and cost £12,000 to build in 1846, was paid for almost entirely from his own pocket, a mere £1,000 coming from the parish rates.

Similarly, the vicarage where he once lived – West Meon House, at the

play host to the village fêtes and summer performances of Shakespeare performed by the active village theatre group, the West Meon Players.

It is said that Bayley built such a fine rectory 'so that no-one but a gentleman could be rector of West Meon.'

Today the beautiful cottages and houses clustered around the two sides of the Meon stream are certainly fit for any of the gentlefolk aspiring to live in a truly beautiful Hampshire village. West Meon and its fascinating, if sometimes mysterious history, really are priceless.

bottom of the village – is a grand building, whose expansive grounds

Tender 2008